Dentists

by Mari Schuh

BELLWETHER MEDIA · MINNEAPOLIS, MN

Note to Librarians, Teachers, and Parents:

Blastoff! Readers are carefully developed by literacy experts and combine standards-based content with developmentally appropriate text.

Level 1 provides the most support through repetition of high-frequency words, light text, predictable sentence patterns, and strong visual support.

Level 2 offers early readers a bit more challenge through varied simple sentences, increased text load, and less repetition of high-frequency words.

Level 3 advances early-fluent readers toward fluency through increased text and concept load, less reliance on visuals, longer sentences, and more literary language.

Level 4 builds reading stamina by providing more text per page, increased use of punctuation, greater variation in sentence patterns, and increasingly challenging vocabulary.

Level 5 encourages children to move from "learning to read" to "reading to learn" by providing even more text, varied writing styles, and less familiar topics.

Whichever book is right for your reader, Blastoff! Readers are the perfect books to build confidence and encourage a love of reading that will last a lifetime!

This edition first published in 2018 by Bellwether Media, Inc.

No part of this publication may be reproduced in whole or in part without written permission of the publisher. For information regarding permission, write to Bellwether Media, Inc., Attention: Permissions Department, 5357 Penn Avenue South, Minneapolis, MN 55419.

Library of Congress Cataloging-in-Publication Data

Names: Schuh, Mari C., 1975- author.
Title: Dentists / by Mari Schuh.
Description: Minneapolis, MN : Bellwether Media, Inc., 2018. | Series: Blastoff! Readers. Community Helpers |
    Audience: Age 5-8. | Audience: K to Grade 3. | Includes bibliographical references and index.
Identifiers: LCCN 2017036494 (print) | LCCN 2017042148 (ebook) | ISBN 9781626177444 (hardcover : alk.
    paper) | ISBN 9781681034454 (ebook) | ISBN 9781618913050 (pbk. : alk. paper)
Subjects: LCSH: Dentists–Juvenile literature. | Teeth–Care and hygiene–Juvenile literature. | Mouth–Care
    and hygiene–Juvenile literature.
Classification: LCC RK63 (ebook) | LCC RK63 .S3825 2018 (print) | DDC 617.6/01–dc23
LC record available at https://lccn.loc.gov/2017036494

Editor: Nathan Sommer   Designer: Brittany McIntosh

Printed in the United States of America, North Mankato, MN.

Table of Contents

At the Dentist

The dentist shines a light into Addy's mouth. He checks Addy's teeth.

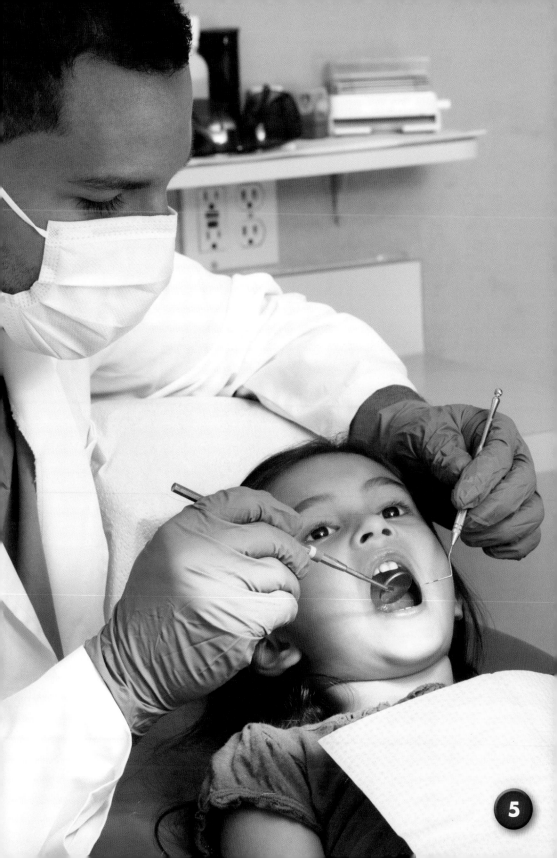

The dentist teaches her how to brush and **floss**. Then, he gives Addy a new toothbrush!

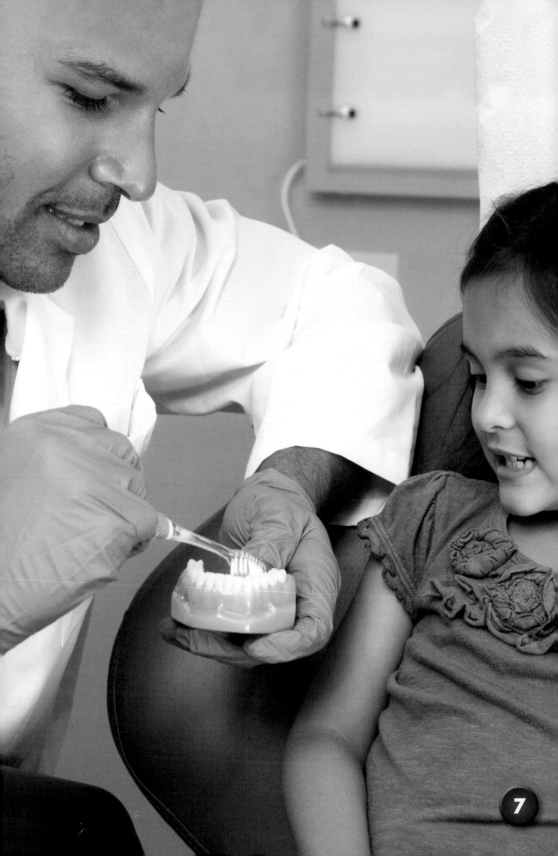

What Are Dentists?

Dentists are doctors who care for teeth and **gums**. They help us keep our mouths healthy.

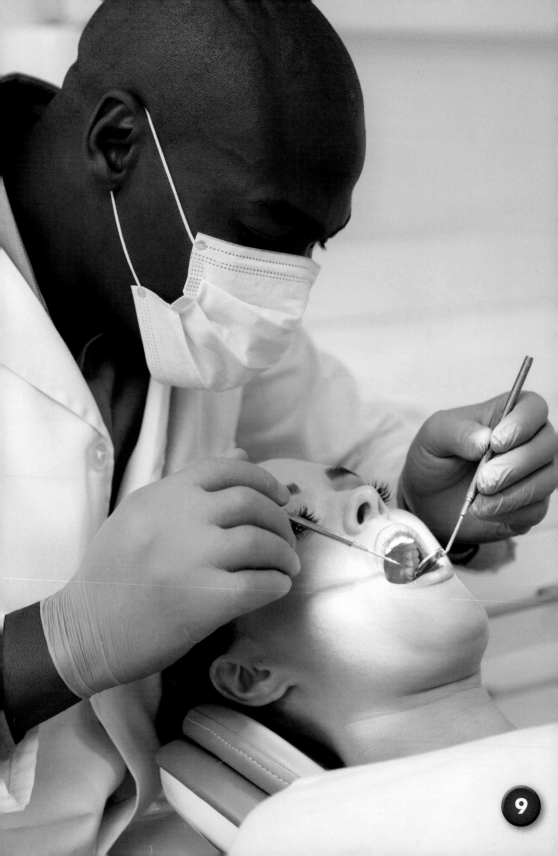

Dentists work in **dental offices**. Some have their own businesses.

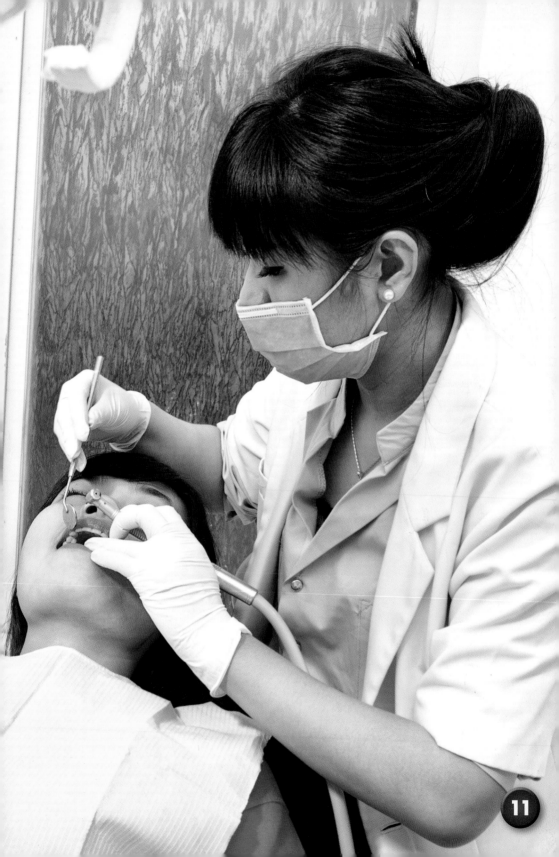

What Do Dentists Do?

Dentists teach **patients** how to care for their teeth and gums.

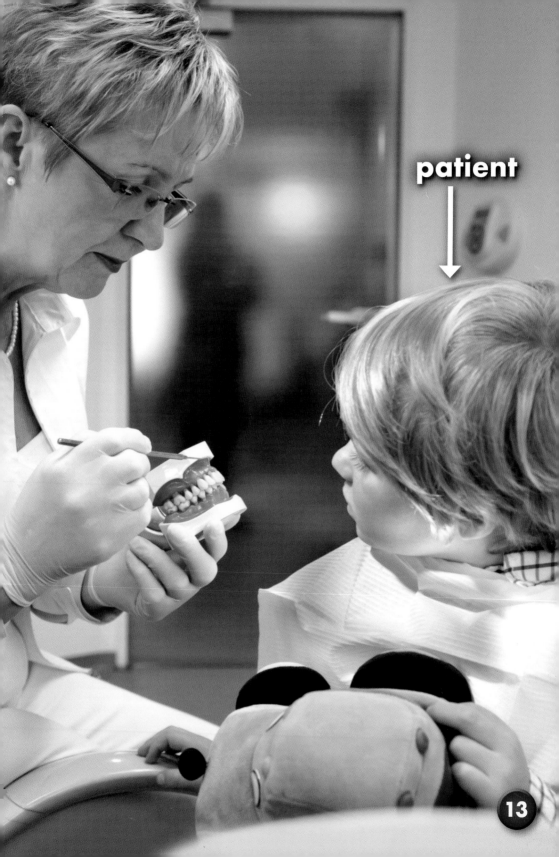

patient

Some dentists fix or remove broken teeth. Others straighten teeth with **braces**.

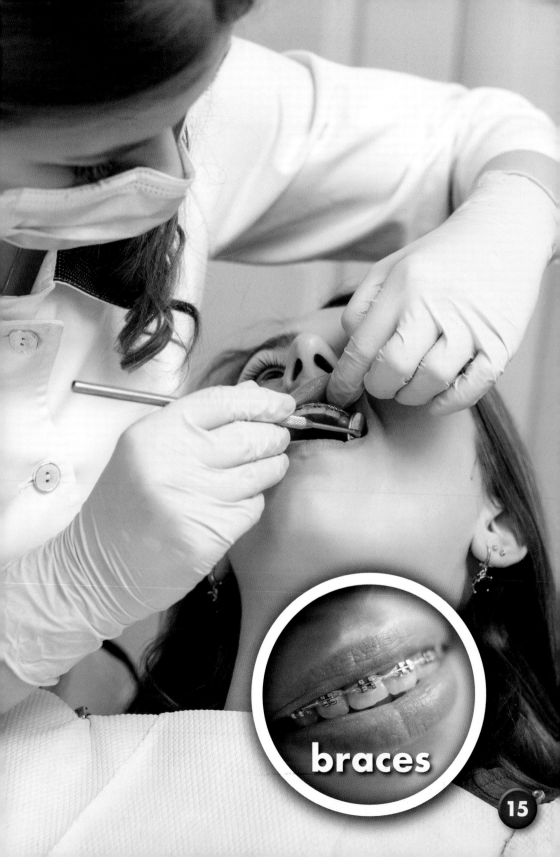

braces

Dentists take
x-rays to see
inside teeth.
They also fill
cavities.

Dentist Gear

mouth
mirror

rubber
gloves

mask

safety
glasses

x-ray

What Makes a Good Dentist?

The mouth is a small space. Dentists must be careful!

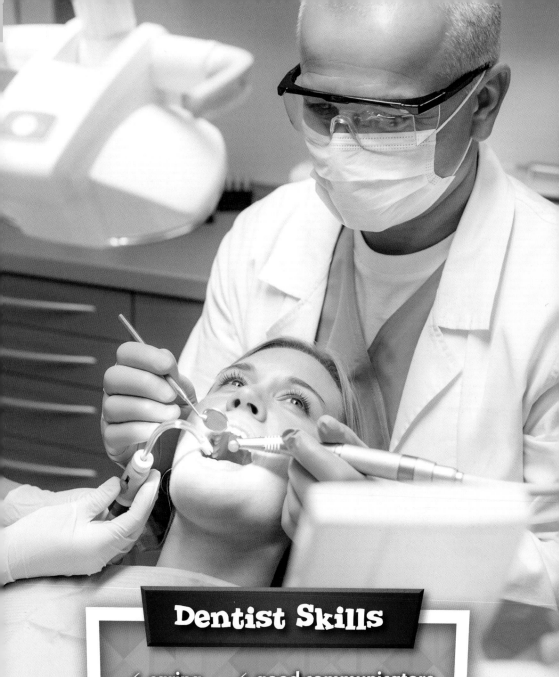

Dentist Skills

- ✓ caring
- ✓ careful
- ✓ good communicators
- ✓ good with people

Dentists are also caring. They make patients feel safe. They give them great smiles, too!

Glossary

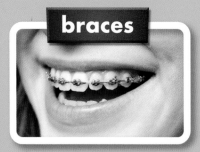

braces

gear attached to teeth to straighten them

floss

to move a thin, waxy thread in between teeth to clean them

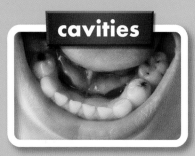

cavities

holes in the teeth

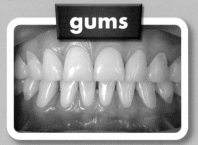

gums

the skin around a person's teeth

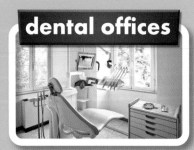

dental offices

places where dentists care for patients' teeth

patients

people in need of dental care

To Learn More

AT THE LIBRARY

Lee, David. *My Visit to the Dentist.* New York, N.Y.: PowerKids Press, 2017.

Less, Emma. *Dentists.* Mankato, Minn.: Amicus Readers, 2018.

Meister, Cari. *Dentists.* Minneapolis, Minn.: Bullfrog Books, 2015.

ON THE WEB

Learning more about dentists is as easy as 1, 2, 3.

1. Go to www.factsurfer.com.

2. Enter "dentists" into the search box.

3. Click the "Surf" button and you will see a list of related web sites.

With factsurfer.com, finding more information is just a click away.

Index

The images in this book are reproduced through the courtesy of: Lucky Business, front cover, p. 22 (bottom right); Syda Productions, pp. 2-3; Monkey Business Images, pp. 4-5, 6-7; michaeljung, pp. 8-9; otnaydur, pp. 10-11; Claudia Paulussen, pp. 12-13; anatoliy_gleb, pp. 14-15, 15 (photo bubble); India Picture, pp. 16-17; urfin, p. 17 (mouth mirror); Mtsaride, p. 17 (mask); Ivaschenko Roman, p. 17 (safety glasses); Africa Studio, p. 17 (rubber gloves); CandyBox Images, pp. 18-19; RossHelen, pp. 20-21; auleena, p. 22 (top left); Vanatchanan, p. 22 (center left); tommaso lizzul, p. 22 (bottom left); Voyagerix, p. 22 (top right); vetkit, p. 22 (center right).